THIS
UNTAMABLE
LIGHT

THIS UNTAMEABLE LIGHT

LUCY GRACE

POETRY CHAPEL
PRESS

Copyright © Lucy Grace 2023.

All rights reserved. No part of this publication may be reproduced, distributed, or transmitted in any form or by any means, without prior written permission of the respective author.

Author website: www.lucy-grace.com
Author email: iamlucyagrace@gmail.com

Poetry Chapel Press
Brisbane, QLD, Australia

Cover Illustration and line drawings: Copyright © 2023 Eliska Kira Kirova, www.kirasheart.com.

Also available in eBook and Audiobook

This Untameable Light / Lucy Grace. -- 1st ed

ISBN 978-0-473-68056-5

For my daughter, Rose.
You are the light that lives inside everything.
Thank you, for birthing me.

In honour of my mother, Heather.
Your unconditional love lives through me,
and runs through every word I write.

Foreword

Lucy Grace is a torch bearer of our time. She is a leader and a teacher of the bravest path I believe a person can walk—the path of the spirituality of inclusion. This path brings divinity into the body, into all of the human experience.

Rather than do the same old thing of using spirituality to create another hierarchy of rejection that makes all human emotions subjugated outsiders while elevating and making superior all that is immaterial and invulnerable, Lucy Grace transmutes the pain of separation into wholeness.

Through this humble and holy process, her embodied alchemy brings heaven to earth.

Lucy energetically affirms that in essence we are luminous beings, essentially healthy, happy and whole and eternally worthy of love and acceptance. She resonates with the wild grace of authentic Love. Her brilliant, courageous heart has learned the warrior art of dissolving through acceptance all that stands in the way of its openness.

I speak about Lucy first before addressing her poetry because her poetry is an emanation of her being. This book is filled with rays of her radiance.

More than a mere sharing of words, a poem is the gift of the transference of the inspired state of the poet to the reader. Lucy's poetry is inspired energy work. Not just a short-lived spark like an ember that just as soon dissolves back into the night, true poetry can have a profound and lasting impact on consciousness.

Lucy is a true poet, an open vessel through which shimmering grace flows. And a poem from this kind of poet, more than a pleasant arrangement of words, is a portal. With unseen genius it can open the reader to a long-hidden light or awaken an unnoticed truth. Poetry from the right source is arguably one of the most potent vehicles for transformation.

To be in the presence of Lucy Grace is to be in a cascade of sunlight. Some immature or fragmented representations of light can act as coping mechanisms for the avoidance of our darkness. But in the case of Lucy Grace, she is a light house that does not avoid the dark but helps us wisely navigate through it. She represents not only a lofty light but a deep light that shines like a beacon toward the integrated way that humanity is moving.

It is my great honor to celebrate This Untamable Light. This book is alive, sewn with seeds of inspiration ready to revivify its readers. This Untamable Light will offer relief to your ravaged heartache, empower your truest essence, and will be a guide that invites you home to the force of light within you that is incorruptible, ever-abiding and ours to cherish and reclaim.

Chelan Harkin, best-selling author and poet of *Susceptible to Light, Let Us Dance! The Stumble and Whirl with The Beloved and Wild Grace.*

Introduction

What does it mean to live a human life? One deeply infused and tended by spirit.

We are moving through a time of great change. Spirituality is in the streets. It's no longer reserved for the scholar, the sage, for men in caves. There's a riot happening. A reformation. We are reclaiming the bone, breath and marrow of spirituality. We are redefining God.

We are entering the womb of all that we are, to spin flesh around spirit, so that it may move as itself—here, lighting the world with its might.

This is deep, sacred, cellular remembering.

Spirituality that does not seek to leave anything out—least of all this reality—but nor is it solely of it. That is not trying to transcend the gift of our humanity, but is wise enough to revere the wisdom of it.

We are learning to let our ultimate selves, guide and tend the human in its suffering and its joy, ushering the fullness of all that we are into this world. Informing our movements, intentions and experience—here. Deepening trust, gratitude, patience, equilibrium, compassion, courage, love.

We are all students. All teachers.

We all know, in our deepest heart—and equally, we all know nothing.

We are learning that heaven is a state; it's around us, within us, above us, below us. It's what we are. The pulse of existence is calling for a spirituality that is not subtly (or overtly) punitive or detached, but that honours the sacred process and anoints the sacred mess of our humanity—in balance with the beauty of all the ways that we are so much more than human. Not favouring one over the other (as if we could). Not denying or pushing away any part of life's wisdom.

No longer do we choose between intelligence or intuition. Reverence or irreverence. The transcendent or the human. The mystical or the mundane. Wholeness inherently includes all. One homed, sacred thing.

The minute we try to leave anything out, we have entered the realm of duality. The self is lovingly included. The body is included, pain is included. Power, joy, apathy, fear, grief, all included.

The perfection of nature—of expansion and contraction—of sacred process, is all recognised and included.

Here, light and dark are not binary, each exists within the other. And each acts as a portal to deepen our capacity for expansion.

No longer do we shun parts of ourselves we deem too broken to be "good" or "spiritual." We know it's all spiritual. Every part of us, every slug, every orphan, every wild dog in us—is brought home to love.

And love, is the intelligence required.
Love is the input, and greater love is the output.
Not a saccharine, fluffy, boundaryless love. But a mighty, homed, deeply powerful love. Able to move mountains or stand for armies if needed. And it will be needed, at times.

We are all healers and the healing. We are all gurus, kings, beggars and thieves.

Grace moves us along, through sacred process, through the alchemy of flesh—turning our suffering to gold and gifts for the world.

We are not required to white knuckle our lives, or cut and paste our personalities to be better, be more, be enough.

We do not need to earn the love of a tyrannical God who lives in the clouds adorned in white robes. We are loved by all of life, simply because we exist.

It's time to redefine God.

God is our dearest friend, a beggar, a deeply loving mother, a whirling dervish, or whatever we want It to be.

God, consciousness, life-force, Allah, Great Spirit, boundless awareness, whatever you want to call it—call it by any name—loves us so much it'll fit in whatever box we put it in. And when we're ready to expand our view of it, it'll come out of all boxes and show us just how unbound it is. Just how unbound, we are.

Existence is limitless.

It is not bound to any tradition, religion, idea, concept or framework that we try to impose on it. There are no rules, no criteria to gain entry, and no one is excluded.

All traditions, rituals, practices and religions are welcomed—insofar as they lead us closer to the truth of ourselves, and help us to become more loving, more authentic and more whole human beings.

So much of ego-bound spirituality today, seeks to separate. To render "my way" superior. The arrogance and defense in that, can only belong to a self in fear.

We only exclude—ourselves, or anyone else—from the unconditional love of life, to the degree we are in fear. Perhaps of our own inadequacy or inherent brokenness, or of "getting it wrong."

In truth, there are a million ways to pray…and way, leads onto way. The body of God is everything. We cannot get it wrong. There is nothing separate, bound or superior about existence. We only limit this, as far as we are limited. Life loves us deeply, exactly as we are.

LIFE IS THE PATH

A seed eventually blooms into the most beautiful flower. But first it must break down, crack open, travel through mud without any guarantees and give over to instinct and the will of existence.

It does not know there is light through the mud of growth. It does not know its dismantling will lead to its blooming: but it follows impulse. It follows the sacred mess of nature. And God is that mess. We are that mess. Intelligent mess.

We cannot scream at the seed to "bloom!" before it is time. It needs water, sunlight, patience. And when it is ready, it opens.

Nor can we scream at ourselves to "open!" "Heal!" Or "surrender!" We can only meet what is truly here now, deeply and earnestly, and choose to keep opening to what is, trusting life's innate intelligence.

Our unfolding is happening in perfect timing.

Like the seed, we bend, we break, we rise—and through it all, Grace.

Once we come to experience life as the deep benevolence it is—the wonder and magic of existence fills us, we can let go of control and see through the arrogance and limitation of a human mind, thinking it could know anything.

"God" loves every single hair on your head, exactly as you are. "Spirituality" is inclusive of all parts of you, the profound and the profane. The humiliating and the holy.

From this place—from this grace—contractions and fears ease and eventually let go, allowing us to fall ever more deeply into surrender, into deep light—so that it may infuse and tend the human experience, grounding God, through you, here.

This is where we find the intersection of spirit and matter. The divine, everywhere.

So lay down your burdens. Take off your masks. Here is a hearth for you to rest. Here is a God who loves all of you—no matter what you are, aren't, do or don't do.
Here are friends who see through the sacred mess of you—into the might, untamable light, and truth you always are.

And in doing so, call it ever more deeply forth.

If this book finds its way to you and you find meaning in it, I would love to hear what these poems have stirred in you. You can contact me through my website at lucy-grace.com. Here, you'll also find information about my work as a Spiritual Guide, Awakening Mentor and Holistic Therapist. You can join our online community, in-person retreats and find the latest poetry and courses.

In loving service,

Lucy

TABLE OF CONTENTS

GREAT SPIRIT 2

SUMMER ASHRAM 4

THE GODS WANT TO DANCE 6

WE MUST FOLLOW THE CANDLE IN OUR HEARTS 8

THERE IS NO SYNAGOGUE 10

GRACE 12

IMPACT 15

LOVE POEM (FOR INFINITE INTELLIGENCE, GOD, CONCIOUSNESS-WHATEVER YOU WANNA CALL IT) 18

IRREVERENCE 21

.... 22

OH KEEP YOUR GOD 23

ON NOT KNOWING, NOT LEAVING, NOT REACHING 27

NON-DUALITY? 30

WHEN I NEED SOUND HEALING 33

THE ONLY PRAYER 36

DAVID BOWIE 39

IF THERE'S AN "I" 42

MY GOD 43

KAIROS TIME 46

ANOINT EVERYTHING 48

THERE'S ONLY ONE TEACHER 54

PROVIDENCE (FOR THE BELOVED) 55

PRESCRIPTION 56

AWAKENING 64

MY "SPIRITUALITY" IS IN THE STREETS	66
NOTES FOR BEING HUMAN	70
BENEDICTION	73
I WENT TO GOD ON MY KNEES	75
GROUND	76
TODAY I FELT TENDER	78
WE HAVE TO WALK OUR WARS	80
SOMETIMES LIFE CALLS US TO LET GO	83
"TODAY IS A GOOD DAY TO DIE"	85
SOMETIMES	88
ALWAYS, NEVER.	89
ALL THIS, LIGHT (CHILDHOOD)	91
WE BREAK OUR HEARTS	92
GOODBYE TO FRIENDS (THE GRIEF OF AWAKENING)	94
MAYBE THERE'S GRACE	95
I FIND MYSELF IN YOU	100
SISTERS	102
THE FLOOD OF YOU	103
MY MOTHER'S LOVE	105
SHE KNEW, HE KNEW	108
ON LOVE, LIGHT	110
ALL THESE HARD, HOLY THINGS	114
AS IF OUR HEARTS LIVE INSIDE OF US	120
GRACE	121
FORGIVENESS IS	124
SOMETIMES	125
MY TEMPLE	127

I'VE BEEN THINKING ABOUT	128
DON'T YOU SEE?	130
COURAGE (NEW LIFE)	131
YOUR BODY IS NATURE	132
I WENT TO GOD ON MY KNEES	135
ON BEAUTY	136
ONCE WE WERE WARRIORS	137
THIS IS FIERCE GRACE	140
WE MEET THE GURU IN LIFE	142
A WOMAN'S BODY	144
WHEN WE SEE THE GOOD	147
PRAYERS	150
THANK YOU	152
MY DEEPEST WORK	155

Lucy Grace

Deep Light

GREAT SPIRIT

Move me.

Return me
to the borders of my body,
that you may take me
where you want me.

Work through me.

Use my hands,
these feet,
this tongue,
the sweat from this brow.

Take any humble skill
I may have, for your work.

Colonise my heart with your love,
that I may bring heaven to earth
through these cells—NOW.

That I may fill the world
with understanding, kindness,
compassion—not wait for some
other body to do it.

Infuse me.

Let me lead with love, even within
the tyranny of my own humanity.
Let me BE your humility, walking.

Imbue me.
I am wholly, completely,
devastatingly

yours.

SUMMER ASHRAM

We don't need to dress up
our spirituality in fancy language.

Sanskrit might as well be cicada hum.
Church is apple blossom and watermelon.

Choir is a chorus, from a bank of summer
flowers worshiping sky. Our sacred drum is
wailing children stomping sand

I am
      and am
            and am.

I get my sermons from slugs.

I am schooled by sea-glass, and the alchemy
of lifetimes of broken hearts.

I am, more than human.

And if I can't trust when I'm scared,
then how can I say I trust?

If I can't love—here—when things fall apart
then I can't say I truly love.

If peace inside of me, relies on peace
outside of me—it's not peace.

I am.
Majesty and algae.

I am "spirituality."

No robe needed. No green smoothie.
No temple. No costume.
No "channelling." No "download."
No archetypes. No exclusive circles.
No animal skull/fancy dress/skin drum
can emulate, or replace this.

We are
and are
and are

limitless.

*

There's no guru, but your own breath.
So don't kiss my feet
and feed me sugar,

let's lie in the long warm grass
and worship all the light
we can and cannot see

together.

THE GODS WANT TO DANCE

To be known
from the ground, up.

Flame through limbs
from the fire-pit in my guts.

Drum an altar in the
temple of my heart.

This holy inhabitation
like a full poetic laugh.

And. So. I. Dance.

Wet
    feet
        stomping

seeds deep
into the fertile dirt
of my light-dark heart.

Hips rounding,
honouring the drum

breasts
legs
laugh

I AM.
Offered up.
This, sacred thrust
a full-body prayer,
deep homing here.

Let learned people, learn.
Let them overthink.
Let them talk and
trade emptiness like it's currency.

I'll be in the garden
worshiping stars,
devoted to mud,
on my knees
to innocence and sun

because the Goddess IS

she cannot NOT,
know you by the lick of you.

She is the drummer
AND the one who follows

and you could never,
ever know this

until you know,

until she bites you open
and breathes you home.

WE MUST FOLLOW THE CANDLE IN OUR HEARTS

For no other reason
than the light dims
if we don't.

We do know,
its quiet sway
its softening
its tender wick.

Flame language.

We do know,
when we're ignoring
its messages.

Besides, if the path
is sure—it's probably
someone else's.

But turning off, into hedgerow,
into bracket, into the wilderness
of our hearts' whispers,
is a quiet kind of courage.

No standing ovation.
No cheering crowd.

Just a tumble-weed knowing

and the deep-hearts, soft laugh
—if we're lucky.

*

All these hard, holy things!
They can't bury us,
because we are seeds.
They simply ask us
to open wider-still
and choose
love.

And the harvest
of our hearts is
everyone's.

THERE IS NO SYNAGOGUE

No cathedral
no temple
no church

but my own heart.

Wherever I go
I carry that.

Heaven is here,
in hip-sway,
it's a state.

It's the realm of light
and vibration
around us, within us
above us, below us.

My breath
is my sacred text
bellying me home,
reminding me
of the wisdom of
silence and echo.

I drink Christ's blood
from the chalice
in my own heart,
offer myself up
on the altar of "yes."

Sacrament

is the tenderness
of this pain, stripping
everything away,
burning me deeper
into trust.

Let me commune
with the trinity
of faith, fierce grace
and this chestful of

love.

GRACE

We bound our feet back then
with ache and myth, stumbled
and bled and hoped and wept.

The churches had hard stone floors
and held people with hard stone faces
and our knees longed to land in the
softness of an earth that could cradle us,

our hearts ached to open to a God
who could see our goodness.

We longed for holding, benediction
that was demand-less, we longed to
lay down our armour and rest.

We're on a pilgrimage of flesh
all the way out here, so far
from the home we had at God's breast.
We need kindness, softness,
the sanctuary of breath.

There's nowhere else to go.
This is the womb. This is the
only cathedral, and it's Grace.

Not intelligence.
Not uncommon sense.
Not ideas and etchings on
sepia maps. Not arguments
about rightness and wrongness
and wholeness or less-ness or
is-ness and isn't-ness.

Lucy Grace

Not ideas about which path is best.

It's all Grace, and Grace is experienced
that's why we took up flesh
—that we may bend, break, rise,
dance, howl, long, kiss, know ourselves
as compassion, impatience
impermanence.

There is no pilgrimage
but that into our own blazing chests.

The walk from penance to remembrance
is through opening arteries and making
the sweetest love, with our own breath.

*

There is nothing to atone for.

When we see madness, grief
sadness—wrestle—in ourselves or another
it's only pain moving, it's not proof
of all the ways we're unworthy
of a God, or a life that demands perfection.

Don't you see? God, is a slug too.
She wove mucus and stars
from the same thread
and stars burn themselves out
just to carve a heart for your chest.
Wisdom sees, perfection everywhere.

*

We sing and grieve all at once.

My hand has always held yours.
Your heart has always wed mine.

You know this, as well as I do.

But what are words between friends?
The tides speak language enough.

There
is
no
pilgrimage

but the slow disrobing
of our beautiful, blazing hearts.

IMPACT

I try to be
as unbusy
as I can be.

Business
hurts me.

Leaves no time
for receiving.

No space

for a breeze
to waft through

and stoke
the embers in me.

I need air around me,

silence
to bow before
crickets chorusing.

Stillness
to allow wisdom to
root-in deeply.

Why we insist
on believing

that wholeness
exists in adding
is beyond me,
subtracting
is deep life
love-making,
savouring, marinating.

Let culture keep its busy,
it's not importance:
it's impotence.

Everyone spread so thin
they forget the "I am."

The wisdom of
pleasure and silence.

I'll be outside listening
to trees teaching
on the intelligence
of dew and matter.

I'll be inhaling deeply
the gnosis of
butterfly wing flutter.

I'll be opening, filling
RECEIVING ether,
before erupting as
Her fire.

*

Only then
will I burn through town,
ignite streets, disperse crowds,
take signage down.

Move paper—reverently—
from one side of the
factory, to another.

DO. Wholly, completely,
before unbecoming
fire.

Before returning to being
(ember).

LOVE POEM (FOR INFINITE INTELLIGENCE, GOD, CONCIOUSNESS- WHATEVER YOU WANNA CALL IT)

The lines of a lifetime gather like water.
In you, I saw a billion lives
merging, melting, tumbling together.
The current of us lapping
our jagged angles to sea-glass,
smooth and brightly sun-drunk.

You were always so unsober,
a whirling pool of eddys and saltwater
and we went under, for each other.

Breath-tides mined
in the moonlit ocean bed
of my heart and mind.

Besides, we all have to start
and end somewhere —or nowhere—
depending on who's looking—and how,
whose praying (and how)
whose touching ... and how.

And oh! The rocks in us.
The before and the after of us.
Our edges smoothing along the way,
blunt instruments taking their toll

but I know you so well,
your heart is a carnival carved
of river-mud and spells.

Kingfishers sing, brightly and deeply
from inside the well of you.

And for so long we ghosted
the banks of each other,

until we didn't.

Until tidal waves couldn't stop us.
Until memories and merging's
and all we are, couldn't be contained
by banks, or damns, or natures plans
—we are that. So we let ourselves
spill the banks, because what else is there?
But this

one
precious life.

No king-tide, no water-tight plan
can undo what is. What we are.

And your salt-skin
is no longer a wound-rub
but a salve, that homes itself here
in a current of bone marrow and breath

and I will love you
as fiercely
as the river runs to the sea
as deeply
as you have always loved me.

For just as nature
finds rest in being
exactly what it is,

so too have we.

*

Come, sit.
Let me feed you sugar.
Let me wash your aching feet,
for we are,
         we.
River and sea.
Everything, nothing.

You, me.

And God is here
in your beautiful
broken heals,

this is worship.

Let me kiss
the mud of you,
it is simply the mud of me,

perfectly, precisely
infinitely wisely,
we.

IRREVERENCE

I know descension
happens in moments
but I've always been
in love with irreverence.

There's something so joyful
—so utterly holy—

about the cheek of
rising from praying,
only to allow the human
her swearing.

I have it on good authority
God doesn't mind,
She loves

all of me.

'Yeshuu' by Robby Donaghey
Used with Permission

OH KEEP YOUR GOD

That doesn't say fuck
and holds her breath worrying
what other people will think.

My God is dancing to Bowie
under moonbeams.

Your God can keep her starched collar
and perfect blow-dry.
My God is flinging mud pies,
sky high on love of this one
miraculous life.

Last time I saw her my God was
knee-deep in the pig pen squealing
along with a new litter,
I don't even bother to call her in to tea
she'll mince in when she's ready.

Keep your Gods of perfect branding
perfect colour schemes
perfect photoshopped pictures

my God is in the kitchen of joy
celebrating her love-lines with
clumsy selfies and a marriage to
the truth of her.

Your God can keep her thigh gap
(her WHAT?!)—mine is worshiping
love that doesn't measure, require, compare
or suck the life-force out of its object
of desire—in order to desire it.

We've been rolling around in the hay gleefully
while your God was measuring calories,
preening, perfecting and judging the joy
right out of you, ironing freedom
into straight lines and telling pallid bible stories
with all the good bits taken out.

Your God bores me to tears
with her toxic 80's "positive thinking."

I couldn't even stifle the yawn
at how small and safe her talk was—she's
terrified of herself, thinks she can manicure out
all the wobbly, holy, delicious parts.

Christ save us (no actually, somebody get
Jesus over here, we need his bullwhips
or his willingness to overturn tables.)

This holy emergence
is alive with blood and the
fleshy radiance of the cosmos.

I'm all in, and so is my God,
so we must be off—we've a date
to howl at the moon and be pulsating,
alive, creatures of light who dance in the night
and besides—your God has a date at some fancy
exercise studio that smells like cleaning products
and expectations, early in the morning
so you better retire together
and when you get bored of her

we'll be in the garden eating stars
and dancing to the third encore of the night
—after which we'll be sitting quietly
holding hands and feeling the sanctity
of quiet-breath in our chests and
the chorus of crickets anointing
everything—all of the cosmos
and all of us

hoping you might come join us,
and if you do, my God will hold out
her arms, bear hug you and say:

"What took you so long? This party
wasn't the same without you
—ditch that dullard and let's dance!"

**

NOTE: when I speak here of "your God" I don't mean actual Gods.

Everyone's God deserves respect, and there is (of course) no such thing as "your God and my God" – it's all one thing, no matter how we might prefer to imagine it.

Life force/consciousness/God loves us so much, it'll be whatever we need it to be and there is room here, for everyone's God.

I use the word "God" as metaphor for all the things we give our attention, time and heart to. All the things we lend our strength, and the light of our awareness to.

I speak about the things we place between God, and us. Our addictions, our fears, our safe habits that disconnect us from the wild messy—whole—truth of us, and the gorgeous imperfect truth of others. The ways we play safe. The protections we create, that become prisons.

The dead things we worship, like ideas about what others may think, or beauty standards imposed on us by a dysfunctional culture.

We give ourselves away to these things—our precious time is squandered and before we know it, the years have gone by and we haven't danced much, connected much, or really come to know what it means to be free and deeply, authentically us.

What if we gave ourselves permission to expand into the fullest version of ourselves? To become deeply human, through being more than human?

Somewhere under the rubble of All These Useless Things—the fleshy radiance of ourselves and one another waits to be found, resuscitated—revealed and revelled in.

ON NOT KNOWING, NOT LEAVING, NOT REACHING

This is wholeness.
And what I am, is
perfect brokenness.

A swell of wild flowers,
bursting stems, overflowing heads,
thorns, and the sweetest scent.

Sacred mess.

Untameable precision.
Some kinda perfection.

Wholeness is
no other moment to reach for.
No addition, no oblivion,
no new note to strive for.

No romance that would
ever mean more
                love
than what is already here
-in me, of me.

No holding
no seeing
no meeting

that would allow me
to touch God
more completely.

Maybe God is in the gaps,

in the subtle terror
of our humanity,
the mud between
the bricks—mortar.

Maybe it's not the prayer
but the way our knees
kiss earth as we make it.

Maybe God is so omnipresent,
so magnificent, She IS the mediocrity
of me, as well as the melody.

Maybe She's so mighty
She can stomach all of it
and more, no need to seek
elsewhere things.

Maybe, God is so holy
He doesn't need
to leave
        anything.
IT IS
and
I AM

the sacred ordinary.

*

Finding God is always right here,
between my toes, if I can be so bold
as to stop, look, rest and un-know.

Otherwise it's all just reaching
for some other moment, some other idea.

Maybe God IS this dread
simmering in the pit of our guts,
this quiet fear that we are all
completely fucking it up.

Our sepia-toned incoherent
human suppleness—maybe that's God, too.

And must we rush? To know, to add,
to fix, to do? To cover up this, now.

Maybe it's all just an endless
cosmic wink.

I AM
(all I ever need to be)

and it is all so utterly perfect, that
the joke has only ever been on the

"me."

NON-DUALITY?

People talk
of being or doing,
of the mountain or the village
as if they are separate.

As if one is flight,
the other fervour.

But there is an
in between place.
Not where the mountain
grows legs and walks sagely
through the village, anointing saints,
building crypts for relics,
steadfastly clinging to its lofty
mountain air, insisting on its special
separate (spiritual) shape,
stubborn over right angles,
sanctifying the "real"
and excluding the "unreal."

But a place where
it can't not know itself
as ether—ignite, become fire.
It can't not erupt into what it
already ALWAYS was,

open so deeply
so unconditionally
so deliciously, as to disappear
and merge liquid-like with the village
not consuming it—as lava would,
but becoming it, too. Gently, no fuss.

A place where mountain melts,
village melts, edges melt, concepts melt,
ideas melt, rightness melts, wrongness melts

and all is:
being
doing
fighting
loving
rallying
celebrating
weeping
praying
opening
opening
opening.

All is dancing.

Just ONE soft
sacred thing.

**

NOTE: non-duality is a loaded word now. We use it to try and convey a felt-sense of union consciousness.

And yet non-duality teachings and concepts can be so dual. In reality, for some—the interpretation/expression of awakening or non-duality is still binary. This (spirit) is real. This (humanity) is not. This is sacred/this is not—which is, by its very nature, dual. There's a split. It's not wholeness if it leaves something out.

The deeper we go, we come to see divinity in everything. We find that liberation is freedom to be cosmic and human. Freedom from all concepts.

The same mechanism that can cling to a self, can cling to a "no self." It's the mechanism that wants seeing through.

Here, we merge spirit and form and find: just the sacred, just the sacred, just the sacred...everywhere.

WHEN I NEED SOUND HEALING

I bathe in cicada hum.
When I need ministry
I let the grass lavish
it's deep devotion upon me
and the dew drip its sermons
right into my heart.

I anoint my feet in puddles
and I praise mud.

I was never alone,
who am I fooling?

I was fathered by mountains,
mothered by ocean,
I was taught by landslides,
and caught by the woman
I became during them.

Stars serenade me
with their chorus of hallelujah's,
offer themselves up as pin-pricks
of wonder and guidance
in the darkness.

Trees salute me, stand
guard and strengthen me,
offer their wisdom—if I'm listening.

I am.
All existence.
My friends are rocks and
praying mantises, I thread
their hearts through mine, like
an endless chain,

let the sky teach me loyalty
to warmth AND shadow
—the humility of hail
and the sanctity of

change.

*

And through it all: love,

ablaze from magma—up
through the soles of me.

I give the Mother
my body, for colonising.

We are ember and water,
all at once, we are
so deeply loved— just like this—
with our limping, broken
hearts, full of fear

we are
        and are
and are

sacred mess, perfect process.
For this, and another thousand reasons

we are blessed.

THE ONLY PRAYER

There is a flow to life
that we must follow,

a place where the mystical
meets the mundane

the profound collides
with the profane

where every butterfly wing
points the same way.

And we can read the runes,
pull another card, scry
our lives all we like, hoping
for a different roll, of the same dice

but we DO know. We know
Graces whisper. Beckoning us
on journeys we wouldn't choose,
breathing us things,
we would rather unknow.

And so, we will go

dancing
or dragged.

Lucy Grace

*

Every day, the same prayer:
"Take these hands, this heart, these
lips—for your work, your words,
I am wholly yours."

And yet, still I can grieve
the things I'm asked to release.

I suppose then there's
only one prayer I ever need
to know, and that is:

*please show me how
to let this go.*

This Untamable Light

Lucy Grace

DAVID BOWIE

Lives inside of me.
He says: "Forget priestessing
—or anything—unless it comes
from the hot guts of you.

This simply is
—no dressing up necessary."

"But you were master
of ceremonies," I say.

And he says "yeah, for joy,
not to claim any one way
but to blow holes in ideas,

cloaking people in roles and rags
only gives them more to hide behind."

"I can't say that to them," I say.
"They'll crucify me, gimme
something more digestible."

And he says: "You really think
it's red pill or blue pill?
All the colours of the rainbow
live inside of you,
do the thing that makes your life
meaningful and joyful—nothing less.

That might be temple arts, Zen,
talking with a dead musician
or walking alone.

The trick is
never make yourself homeless
in your own home.

Your heart, your heart
—your precious heart—
is the only place to go,

no role can ever
supersede letting go."

"Yeah," I say.
"But gimme something concrete.
Bowie, please. These are nuanced ideas
everyone thinks their path is best
they'll get defensive otherwise."

And he says with a wink: "Tell em:
integration—not indoctrination.

Tell them to use whatever serves
them, but to release roles like
they're concrete skin.

If you truly seek
freedom, and wisdom
you'll use ideas and ritual
as inspiration, but I was

Buddhist on Tuesday,
ran magic on Thursdays
and threw it all out on Sunday
to rest in galaxies.

We are all things, and no-thing
the most important thing
is we remain free beings,

we are limitless

human concepts
have subtle ways of binding us

there's nothing to be found
outside of us, that didn't
begin and end within us.

If there's any secret it's that
IT'S ALL ONE PATH

so take it in to your body
only insofar as it truly

expands your heart."

IF THERE'S AN "I"

She is the breath
of the divine

moving as its chest,
its limbs, its heart.

What else could I be?

The body of God
is everything.

I am drunk on this love!

Let empires, towns
the price of gold

fall

God is here, in the dust.

Lucy Grace

MY GOD

Is hilarious.
She puts eels
at the hem of rivers
just to make me wince
because I'm intrigued
and appalled—all at once.

I mean, their slimy sweetness
is just so confusing!

She belly laughs and impels
me to dance life deeply
—no holds barred.

She says: "Open your heart, Lucy
—wider still—give ALL of you and more!"

She sweeps her arms over dew
and flowers and cockroaches and
says: "I made all this, just for you,
what're you waiting for?!"

My God has never left,
not even when I've said mean
or self-centred things
—that's when my God
holds me even more deeply.

"You're not alone." She says,
"Pick up, start again—I'm here
with you always."

My God is constantly telling me
how bright and brave I am,
how utterly in love with me She is.

Sometimes I get so bored with it
I have to swat her away and ask for space
for a bit—"The way you love me is
limitless!" I say, feeling frustrated at
the sheer grace of it, the sheer impossibility
of a love like this.

And she rolls with laughter.
"You'll come crawling back."

But the truth is, I never really
left, and we both know it.

She's all of me.

My God doesn't forgive anything.
She says, "There's nothing to
forgive in the first place,"

and then: "Let's hit the bar, I'll drive,
I heard the angels are playing a gig,
and I still owe you shots from last time."

My God is embarrassingly
smitten with me—warts and all

and She loves you the same way too
—if you'll let Her. She's waiting
like a weirdo just outside your door,
hoping for the tiniest nod from you
—then she'll rush in, scoop you up and say:

"Let's not waste another day
with shame, fear or feeling inadequate
—you're fucking perfect and I'm so glad
you're finally letting me love you."

KAIROS TIME

I open my full hands
before Kairos,
say that holy name and

trust.

I lived my whole life
on a whim and a dime
—on God's time,

found solace
and wonderment
in the light that lives
inside the darkest quiet.

Freedom isn't knowing
all the steps, freedom is
how naked I'm willing to be
as I walk them.

This holy emergence
wants to drop skin and
listen. If I'm too busy
demanding, I can't hear
what wants to happen.

The composition is faith.
The lesson: always
                      love.

We can read other people's
sheet music, and force ourselves
to follow it—or we can burn
the script and

dance.

ANOINT EVERYTHING

It's all holy.

The way your head bows slightly
as you sip tea—some kinda prayer.

The way your breath-filled chest
sups air like wine, like
blood of Christ, as you watch a lady bug
crawl across dust on a forgotten ledge.

THIS is pilgrimage.
No need to leave your front deck.

Listen, while a homeless man blares bile
from his chest across the street
like a sermon.

Honour his strength.

Everything hallowed, everything holy.
He's simply inviting the wild dogs
that live muzzled in you, to be let loose, too.

He's asking you to open, soften,
let them in.

Unlock every cold cage in you
and invite them closer, worship at their paws
—feed them pudding. Wash their snotty snouts
tenderly, saint their feral bodies, before
breathing them, softly home to resting.

*

Walk
your beautiful, blazing heart
a while in silence.

Can you just be here
with whatever sacred mess
pretends to claim you, today?

Let go
       of the white knuckling,
just like a foetus doesn't need
tinkering with to become a baby,
nor does your birthing need "doing"
it's already happening in perfect timing.

And that's not some wan cliché,
that's natures intelligence,
that's sacred process.
We don't need to "figure it out"
life's wisdom does that.

So just walk. Just breathe.

Bless
every
step.

Bless, every piece of gravel
under foot that pierces flesh.

Bless hurt. Bless joy.
Bless the unexpected balloons
that dance through your sky.

Bless grit like its grace.
No more running away—from you.
Because if it's here in our lives: it's grace.
And if it's not here in our lives: it's grace.

So take every barrier between you
and you, and strip it all away.
When we speak of being ONE with
everything this is what we mean:
how deeply can you let it all in?

Absolute intimacy with all existence
—until it becomes us.

Let in: the disappointments,
your perceived inadequacies,
your terror at not knowing
if you're forgotten here,
the horror of your own humanity

the endless wondering
if all your struggles mean nothing
and you won't amount to anything

this dread simmering
in the pit of your guts

the quiet fear
that you're completely
fucking it up
and your own lack
is so obviously mirrored back
in the horrific simplicity of this

one
empty
moment

so you better run and run
from the torture of it.

You better
scroll
eat
shop
improve
add
exercise
buy more land
do another Instagram post
become a leader
of something—anything—
extend
do up the kitchen
source more heroin
(in whatever form that comes in)
could be another spiritual book
or improvement course
could be more conspiracy theories
or a worthy cause to support ... *STOP.*

Just stop.

Be still, in the hollow halls of you.
Open completely, Indiscriminately.

Merge with the unbound truth of you.

This is where you finally find
the God you say
has always eluded you.

*

Anoint everything.

See the courage, the beauty
in simply existing. In being willing
to truly be here—vast enough
to keep saying "yes" to it all.
Nothing exiled. Nothing claimed.
No trying to earn love or protect
from pain—no leaving.

Sanctify this moment.

Let it split you open
like it's the deepest compassion.
because it IS, loves intelligence.

Be fearless—merge with it.
Until there's no space left
between that lady bug

and your breath.

*

This is ONE. This is freedom.
There's really nothing fancy about

liberation.

THERE'S ONLY ONE TEACHER

And the teacher
is always
      here.

PROVIDENCE (FOR THE BELOVED)

I carry Him
in my body.

He moves in me
like air.

Somehow
already there

through all time.

He's inside out.

There's no new moon,
no full eclipse
that could move
the tides of me like this.

This is cellular dancing,
deep remembering,
and it has rendered me

motionless.

PRESCRIPTION

There is deep wisdom,
in knowing the difference
between medicine and poison
in your unique system.

The subtleties of degrees
and dosage, levels
of exposure, absorption.

Consider the skill of the hands
administering it—bedside manner,
the nuances of power.

It's not always the person
who speaks the loudest,
that sees the clearest.

*

We're all clambering for belonging,
to be everything or nothing

but the gift is the combination
of our humanity AND infinite reality.

It doesn't have to be one or the other.

There's a billion ways to pray,
and way leads on to way.

You may not need another "container"
or to dance with mother ayahuasca.

You may not need to channel your
"divine feminine" or the "dark mother"

unless you're called to
—in which case, let it breathe you

but remember this:
how your unique heart breaks open
is found in an unprecise combination
of your own sinew and wisdom,

in the tones of your deepest knowing
—and you DO KNOW.

We are all a kaleidoscope
of imprints, hauntings and subtlety,
of magic mushrooms and alchemy
—so burn other people's talismans,
there is no prescription.

One person's tonic is another's arsenic.

Some talk of dark and light
as if we don't all—already hold all of it.

The ones shouting loudest
about others being unconscious
well, it's all noise—isn't it?

All paths, to the depths of our hearts
are beautiful, useful—let's celebrate them

but it doesn't mean we have to emulate them.

Maybe the one dancing naked around that
fire pit, would actually grow more
in being willing to stay still—intimate—

and maybe not.

There is no inadequacy when we know
we can never know anything.

Life is only ever asking: "Am I opening or closing?"
and that looks different for each body.

Praying can be giving over to God
or simply giving up.

Meditation can be deepening or escaping.

Dancing can be expanding or avoiding
—depending on whose moving.

The point is, evolution doesn't
have a formula, one person's
transforming can be another's hiding

and one person's hiding
can be another's transforming,

the nuance and difference
between running, or growing is FELT

and that's inside-out.

Maybe the one merging easily with
God—transcending to other realms—
actually needs to learn to stay HERE
in this body—live life on this plane.

Or the one committed rigidly to yoga
—would grow more in letting go,
surrendering to flow,

then again, maybe not—the point is
our point of growth is

intimate.

The outside view
can't tell us what is true growth
or joy, for anyone.

My love
you don't have to become a "priestess"
or channel the "goddess"
nor do you have to become nothing
in 40 years of Zen,

you have always been
more than all of them combined.

We are all warriors, teachers, Gods and thieves
—down here it's just a matter of degrees
and your heart knows your unique recipe

so fall-in/fall-out—but follow yourself.

You can train yourself to:
say the "right thing"
do the "right thing"
wear the "right thing"

but "fitting in" is never belonging,
and your system knows it.

Belonging, is only ever being
loved and seen as you truly are
—so home yourself, in your own heart,

and if you do need a question to ask
try: "Am I doing this to love
or to BE loved?"

Reverence
will never be a commodity.

Truth is not currency.

Follow only what feels good and right
in your precious body.

Holy "the brand" is only a fraction
of the magnitude of HOLY.

This
is
limitless

we only limit it
as far as each one of us is limited,

we reduce God, spirit, consciousness—
to what we are.

If a hate-filled man reads the Koran
he'll find words that hate.

If a loving man reads the Koran
he'll find words that love

(and it depends on the day
that's in it, tomorrow
he may find something different.)

We are all, all of it.

There is no containment possible
this vastness always is, was, and will be.

Every
single
thing
is "spiritual."

So if you want to break out
and break open, true freedom
is giving yourself permission
to follow your systems innate wisdom.

We can't outsource this,
it's not forcing ourselves to follow
a script written for us,

and sometimes that script
looks like an Audi and a big house

and sometimes that script
looks like: priestess (or purity.)

You.
Are.
Mighty.

The magnitude of you cannot be
contained in bibles, or florals,
bohemian linen, or the next tattoo

play with those things
enjoy them—do you—
but know, you are all of this
and more—don't listen to the masses
Instagram can't contain this

I'll say it again:

you
are
limitless.

We only ever limit this
as far as each one of us is

limited.

AWAKENING

It feels like birthing.
Like squatting close to earth
raw force opening hips, like breath
pulling spirit, deeper into flesh.

It feels like summoning
the magic of eons through bone,
through follicle, through quark,
through open molecule and

heart.

It feels like throwing back my head,
arching breasts and bellying
the entire cosmos through flesh,

it feels like ROARING as praying,
bare feet pressed to mud, earthing
ocean and making love with moss.

It feels like taking in
every creature crawling,
singing, loaming in me, it feels like

becoming everything.

*

There is an ecstasy in existing
that cannot, will not, be colonised.

There's no sterilising or explaining
this away, there's no taming
the power of ocean, tide, moon,
sorrow, blood, rage, joy, seasons,
with your organised wars. With your
theory, ideas, tidy boxes, wrong-making,
right-making, division.

This is woman's way,
and wombs anoint everything.

This is deep midwifery
for your soul—and you know it.

This is the calculus of your becoming,

the axis of your ending
and every beginning
you have ever longed for.

This is birth AND death
folded in on one another, this
is the untameable pulse
of giving over to

nature.

MY "SPIRITUALITY" IS IN THE STREETS

Union wants to come back around
to know itself as the ground, under
these dancing, fumbling feet.

The novelty IS our humanity.
I have no interest in erasing the wisdom
and deliciousness of gravity.

We come from spirit.
We ARE spirit.
We return to spirit.

But to breathe? What a joy!
To know ourselves
through another's finger lines?

To walk, to eat,
to masquerade as people.

To enjoy the flight and sweet grief
of existence—to let it breathe us.

To choose to keep saying "yes"
to the absurdity and magic of this.

We are. It is.
              What a gift.

We are owed nothing,
yet we're given all this.

*

And yet where my true heart beats
there's no "spirituality" and no street.

No east meets west, no cosmic and human,
no quiet supple movement between two.

Just release. Just one thing.
No sea-glass or sea.
No ground. No feet.

And this paradoxically IS
the luminosity that returns me
to being

poetry moving.

*

I am / and I am not,

such sweet
paradox.

Lucy Grace

Bless the Breaking

NOTES FOR BEING HUMAN

Unclench your fisted heart
and let it break.

Just let it.

Open every door of yourself,
give over deeply,
grant entry to the pain
to seep or soar, to drip
or wave, through
every mistake,

every longing, every wish
to belong, somewhere.

Let your heart break.

Know deeply
every open artery,
every breath, every
broken capillary,

because the real tragedy
is only ever leaving yourself.

YES. Life in its wisdom
wants to be felt. So open

every
single
cell

every moment
wants to be deeply
wholly allowed.

The greatest intimacy
is offering up your body
for life, to live itself
(much harder, more nuanced
than it sounds.)

Turn no visitor away
—whether joy or suffering—
make deep love to them all.

Listen to the whispers calling
Let it in, let it ALL in.

A broken heart, an open heart
is only ever-more awakening.

**

NOTE: when I speak here of a broken heart, I
don't mean the romantic kind (only.)

Life has a billion ways to belly us.
And deep magic occurs when we let ourselves be
broken open.

The supple union, of suffering, faith and
wisdom.

When we think about all the bullets we catch and bury, in this miraculous life. Tiny moments, subtle encounters, big knowings. Healing, meeting, trying, not trying.

The question always seems to be the same: are we opening, or closing?
In this moment… this moment… this moment.

How intimate with every part of life can we stand to be?
The mediocrity. The mundanity. The hurt. The subtle—and overt—brutalities.

As well as the miraculous, the joyful, the magical and the hopeful.

BENEDICTION

Invite the tired children
of your heart home to rest.
Offer them a hearth to warm their feet,
feed them honey and broth.

We can feel so lost
out here in the wilderness
of ourselves, in these unfamiliar
wild-west towns, but if there's one thing
I've learned, it's that love is relentless.

The temple gates are always open
and we'll be sent messengers
and friendships and small
winks from the deep heart of
existence. Whispers, urging us on.
Impelling us to return
to ourselves over and over and offer
the benediction of holding
to all the limping, cast-out parts of us.

There comes a time to turn fearlessly,
spirit-wide, without fuss
and make love with the lepers in our hearts.

We are all unbound wholeness and blaze,
we are also hauntings and grief.
And ALL of these things weave
the intelligence of love
ever more deeply into us.

There is deep grace, in our aching.
Our suffering is not our brokenness
—it's our beauty.

There's unimaginable bounty
in the breaking.

I WENT TO GOD ON MY KNEES

Asked what to do
when I was grieving
and She said:

"grieve."

GROUND

I let the sun solve all the
things inside of me today.

Paid homage to the privilege and
tenderness of grass, offering itself
under my feet,

knelt at the alter of seawater
and memory—baptised you out of me.

We are named and renamed
by ocean, made and unmade in
constellations,

your heart will never be far
from mine.

You will burn here, beyond earth core
and silly human things, like time.

And when my knees are sore
and dry from praying to rearrange
the way of things,

you'll find me giving over
to the current and incandescent force
that lives inside all things.

You'll see me, blessing
the breaking,

from somewhere deep within
the unknowing and the
faith in me.

*

Oh life!
I've always loved you so.

Take this heart of sea glass
and light it through

I offer myself up, to be danced and
danced and danced

by you.

TODAY I FELT TENDER

Soft.
Not like a blazing heart,
more like a child
unsure of her part or place.

But I made a choice
"this too" is me
and it gifts something.

Let me open my heart anyway,
go into the world anyway

and breathe.

I am vast, and if it hurts,
it's okay, I can let that in
—and more.

The important thing
is being absolutely
completely

here

alive in the world
moving as all of me.

We are all haunted,
grace-filled beings,
and we learn to live
with the hauntings.

They make us kinder,
more nuanced,
more compassionate.

Let me be soft in this world
where so much is hard,

where so many
choose to harden,

let me, open.

WE HAVE TO WALK OUR WARS

So we have fodder for our poems.

Not specific bullets, medals
or moments, but wisdom
hard won, found under piles
of abandoned ammunition,

in the smoking barrels
of abruptly dropped guns
and the exhausted relenting
of realising what we've lost,

what we've done.

*

Finally, stillness.
The morning after.

Our eyes scanning
the trenches for miles,

corpses strewn
at loveless angles.

No arm-in-arm song.
No chaser for the road.
No laughter-filled,
long walk home
                    together.

Only the hollow no-note
of emptied hearts, the shocking
humility of seeing what we are,

and aren't.

*

All battlefields
eventually dry up.

We know it from the start.

But somehow, we still
get to each other's hearts.

*

We choose our weapons
one way or another,
depending on our tolerance
for closeness.

Existence expands us,
question by question
as we live the answers.

(And sacred is sacred,
regardless).

*

There's a surrender in grief, a cleansing.
Another immersion-lesson.

Another perfect baptism.

SOMETIMES LIFE CALLS US TO LET GO

Of hope.

Of wanting to move
the tides of our lives, as
our little minds would have it.

We are called to trust.

Doesn't a foetus become a baby
-effortlessly- within the pulsing
of these holy bodies?

Flesh weaves itself around spirit
we don't have to "do" the spinning.

The body of God is everything.

Open your arms as wide as you can
and you won't even begin
to encapsulate it.

"Our" lives are a co-creation
with all existence—not a script we write,
manhandle and force. So the truth is
we lose people, plans and things sometimes.

But we can let go and open,
receive the breath of existence,
learn to move with moon and current,
attune to the pulse of nature,
bend over the fires in us, and listen.

We can read the runes
of our lives, stoke our hearts embers
—when strength is needed.

It's here, thigh-deep
in the sacred mess of life
-we find ground inside to
push against and RISE.

*

Home, is the simmering womb
of our own hearts.

Holy, is never homeless.

So let the great rains, rain deep
like a baptism.

It's all just weather.

Right in the centre
of the joy AND the ache in us,
we find the untameable magic of

wholeness.

"TODAY IS A GOOD DAY TO DIE"

A pilgrim
walks her prayers,

she walks the answer.

Somewhere within the despair
and sweet longing
of being human

the meaning of life
is a rhetorical question

—we answer
with every step.

And we only know life,
if we're willing
to know

death.

*

If we live with curiosity and courage we die over
and over within one life.
Versions of ourselves morph and shape shift.
Bodies buried in the yard of us.

As some Native American tribes were known for
saying "today is a good day to die."

Sometimes we shed skin easily, but so often
there's a wrestle. We don't want to lose things or
people, roles, jobs, places, ideas, shields.

And yet if we don't die to what we WERE, we
can't ever know the fullness of what we ARE.
Like a cicada walking out of an old shell, our
emergence depends on letting go.

Whatever is happening in our lives now
—is the calculous of our becoming.

Nature teaches this evolution and renewal, if we
have eyes to see.

If we want to hold even deeper love, we must
first hold death.
This is profound process. Sacred mess.

And yet we often subtly wrong-make ourselves
or overtly despise ourselves when we're not
feeling pleasant or homed, or certain—always.

As if the sky should always be blue.

As if rain isn't a baptism.

What if all this—the fear, the longing, the sweet sadness, the broken parts, the lost, grieving and confused parts—are nothing more than perfect bounty?

What if we remember to bless
this breaking?

Not as fancy words, but quietly, truly.

SOMETIMES

We have to sit inside our sadness.
Enter the call of loneliness
deeply. Feel the weight of
every mistake, every longing,

every wish to go back and
do it differently.

Sometimes we have to know
ourselves as human.

Hollow ourselves out
on the altar of remembering
we ARE responsible for our choices.

These hands have impact,
and there's humility in that.

ALWAYS, NEVER.

Give him to current, to wind.
Let him go to axis and bend.

Bless his exits and entries, bless
the rivering that carries him.

Bless the hollow-bone of him,
the grit and the grace of him.

Bless his kindness, his madness
his flailing, his strength.

Bless the ache he brings, bless
the severed anchoring of his
(yes/no) holding.

Bless this knowing.

*

We do see, one another.

We are not as invisible as
we like to think. And Grace
can also be a graveyard,

spring flowers growing
in the dark corners, the
withered places in us.

He brought magic and
stardust. Who could
resent him that?

Let me kneel at his tomb,
speak the letters of his name
as blessing, not curse.

It takes work.

**

NOTE: for my father, who left when I was a foetus.

This silhouette of "man"—who lived somewhere on Mars and who I thought I never needed anyway.

For all the bullets we catch and bury, in these precious bodies.

And how those flesh-wounds have a way of seeping, of turning even the fully-here, translucent, in a web of energetic patterns that play out over and over in our lives until they clear.

We all walk our holy wars.
We lead armies of ghosts.
We recreate them again, and
again, and again...until we don't.

ALL THIS, LIGHT (CHILDHOOD)

I found God under
a willow tree littered with
needles and used condoms,

inside the broken homes
of people who know how to hope
better than anyone.

My heart broke open
on rusty swing sets,

church was cicada hum
and empty lunchboxes.

We are more than human.

We are stars
who have never forgotten
burning

in an endless sky.

*

Can we really call it suffering
if it gifts us

all this light?

WE BREAK OUR HEARTS

So that they may open.
Run the gauntlet between
human, and more than human.

Know ourselves as fire and blaze,
and smallness and freeze.

We remember our way back to silence,
most often on our knees—that
through-line to the divine.

I'm in love
              with being humbled.

We were made for this, made to
run soft lips over the wound
—sutures be damned.

*

Truth is quiet, still.

There's a place where
everything falls.

The stories.
The bargaining.
The hustling.
The wrestling.
The trying, the losing.

All that expensive "winning."

Truth is quiet, still.
I hear Her drum in my breath:
stay, don't leave you.

The price we pay
to lose ourselves is high.

But what is here
under addiction
under distraction

when we are naked?
Below nudity?

Truth is so intimate, almost
unbearable, ecstatic/brutal.

We were made for this
—made to connect love
to the ache.

What happens here?
When we are palms-up
tender and say:

"I'm willing to see things
differently, I'm willing to lose
everything."

(Even Him. Even the poetry.)

GOODBYE TO FRIENDS
(THE GRIEF OF AWAKENING)

It settles slowly like snow,
the knowing that it's right you go.

The lightness of the release, you
visit me softly sometimes in dreams.

No hollow song.
No rag-doll arms.
No arm-in-arm, 5am
walk home.

Just what's left: the before
and the after of us.

The rightness
of swallowing gravel.
The perfectness of angles.

Lucy Grace

MAYBE THERE'S GRACE

Beyond anything we could imagine.
Maybe we are so loved
that every single hair
on our heads is known.

Maybe intimacy with all things,
simply means intimacy with all of me.

Maybe I'm more portal than black hole.
More elegance than brokenness
—even with my "broken" parts.

Maybe light and dark are not binary
but live inside each other.

And maybe the stars are trying to tell us this.
That's why they choose to shine
in darkness together.

Maybe I am perfect altitude
between land's end, and heaven's ascent.

Maybe, all that we are
—the broken parts, the weeping parts
the hunched, fevered and knotted parts
the scared-I-can't-love-or-be-loved heart

is exactly why, and how—
we are perfect

love.

*

Bless the breaking.
My love, anoint everything.

If someone wants to leave
—let them. you'll come to see
it's alchemy.

Sometimes Grace feels fierce
because dissolution
is the initiation we need.

Our emergence is
nature's highest priority,
not our comfort.

The real tragedy
is only ever leaving ourselves

so let life burn
what it wants
to the ground of you,

you'll be richer
for the regeneration after.

Nature's intelligence
raises us, in the crucibles
we need,

life is the curriculum,
love, the education

so head high, heart open.

Turn toward the fire
with the deep hearts
perpetual wink and say:
take it all, take what you need.

And then bleed.

A broken heart, an open
heart, is only ever more

awakening.

Lucy Grace

LOVE

I FIND MYSELF IN YOU

And having done so
am made real.

You witness
all the parts of me
into existence,

weave them together, make
the unseen, seen.

This is some kinda
sacred rivering

flowing me purposefully
unto all things.

Quantum physics is right.
Your gaze ushers
the wave of me
into particle,

fleshing me out
somehow,

rendering me
                    realer
than real.

'Ground' by Dan Hillier
Used with Permission

SISTERS

I am held on either side
by your fierce love.

You scaffold my life
in king tides, and sigh
with me in awe when life is
a crystal water sunrise.

In all my life, I have never
known the truth that you inspire
and the courage that you command.

We were formed in the crucible
of street-war, and your fire
has learned to burn what is unneeded
and alchemise lessons into treasures.

You raise the mother of dragons in me.

Sing me to the biggest and boldest
of myself and hold me up
while I take flight.

It's you I reach for, in the dark
when I need reminding of all this,

untamable light.

THE FLOOD OF YOU

We carry the weather of our lives
in love lines around our eyes,
natural eddies and hills,

starlight.

Your raging torrent,
your streams,
channelled a hole
right through me,

I was me, always,
rock, air and gravity

and your light, your
softness and might

somehow
hollowed space in me.

*

The courage and hope
of a thousand hands
clasped in prayer, at the
mouth of a raging sea

please.

The stillness and peace
of the endless ocean underneath.

That's what I see in you
and what you undo

in me.

**

NOTE: we experience many floods, in any given life, don't we? Some feel tidal—inevitable.

Others rage from nowhere, taking us by surprise and pulling the air from us suddenly. Bringing us to our knees in prayer.

Some floods are welcome. Like falling in love, they are a cleansing, a birthing.

There are times we let ourselves drown in the sweetness of loving well.

And if the flood is ravaging, unexpected and painful, like all weather—eventually it subsides. And sodden, yet renewed, we RISE.

MY MOTHER'S LOVE

Taught me about God
(Source, Awareness, Great Spirit
whatever you wanna call it.)

Not "God" her vision: some man
with a beard, welding judgement
like weapon and currency.

No.

That was the God her words taught
and he wanted her on her knees,

bellied
        crawling
atoning.

Listen: her words taught me nothing.
Her love was the education.
SHE was the curriculum.

There was little scarcity to her love.
I experienced enough to trust,

to fall back freely into the arms of love.
And love IS Great Spirit—so she gave me faith.

She breathed God into each of my cells
by loving me more than she hated herself.

Her love was never withheld as
punishment, weapon or message

and please do not imagine benign perfection
we are all the same—human love is cut
with gravel and hauntings,

the places we freeze and undo ourselves,

but she forgave it in everyone else
—even if she couldn't in herself.

*

Everyone said we lived in poverty.
It was them who couldn't see true wealth
is a mother standing quietly by while I
screamed "I hate you" and she held herself:

"I love you—in all your ways and always will."

She taught me God will too, you will too,
life will too, no matter what I am,
aren't, do or don't do.

And what else is there?

Somewhere in my marrow is the sense
that all of life is benevolent

and it loves me like she did, without
exception, without expectation—condition-less.

She gave me unearned-love's freedom,
no life-lines to toe, no scripts to follow.

So who needs dollars and cents?
That's her gift, that's

inheritance.

SHE KNEW, HE KNEW

And he knew, she knew,
and they both knew together

about the ocean.

Waves in motion, us
—watermarks.
More than human.

Layers all the way down
to the abyss.

Infinite stillness.

*

He knew, she knew.

And she knew, he knew
and they both knew together

the wisdom of rivers.

The light that lives inside
the grief of the gift
of being human.

Maelstroms, us.
Baptised to sea glass.

Lucy Grace

ON LOVE, LIGHT

You wouldn't know it by looking at me,
but I'm a first-born Viking.

I'm a dragon slayer, I'm lightning.

I walk, with a sword for a spine
and I host steel immaculately.

Don't you see?
It takes the strength of empires
to choose, to let love colonise me.

It takes the might of armies to open myself
to tenderness this completely.

Far from being delicate, the deepest might
is allowing vulnerability, dismantling
every single defence to open-hearted loving,
is fearlessness walking.

You say you think love is saccharine,
foolish, strategic, fake, naïve, pleasing, easy?

Nah, look again.

Love is the ONLY intelligence required,
and we find it on our knees
broken open in brick dust and suffering

the cockroaches of us, gently cradled
and released—alchemy.

*

If there's one truth I know, it's that joy
is the greatest form of activism.

This love, is pragmatism
                              dancing,
wisdom winking,
and who can see, sees.
(The mind thinks, the heart knows.)

The greatest strength is choosing softness.

Opening every single cell fearlessly
to innocence and sun.
I can, precisely because I AM chain mail.

Love is willingly given
deep, delicious permission
to inhabit me, unravel and rewild me.

I have no interest in dropping this
holy body. I want to home
spirit through flesh, let it
express—here—ever more deeply.

This love breathes me condition-less
doesn't discriminate, is unbound fearlessness.
Needs no exclusive tribe (only community)

no trance
no trend
no palace
no prison
no playbook
no tradition
—NO safety.—

This love is objectless, subjectless existence
and it will love you conditionless.

Never mind light's critics—I choose this.
And I can because existence is

fearless.

*

I AM.
A single conceptless tone
woven with every sound
the cosmos ever sung.

You'll find me worshiping
mud and stars equally.
Nothing exiled—all community.

You can trust me, deeply
but you cannot tame me.

I told you: the human
is the smallest part of me

and she too is wild gravity,
she too is soft-mighty

because love's might needs lightening
to insist on existing here, in a world that
ridicules love, reduces love, sidelines love,
tries to silence love,

yet longs to be splayed open
by a love so true, nothing false is left standing.

This world does not need JUST enlightening.
Light needs the brazen audacity of humans,
being.

Life needs us strong enough, solid enough,
courageous enough to

be
love
moving.

ALL THESE HARD, HOLY THINGS

The grace of being,
and all the ways we
swallow sea.

The sweet tumour of sadness
and apathy, the way humans
discard one another so easily
(but rarely as easily as it seems.)

The way fear shuts us down
when myth and wound
cycle bloodstreams.

*

And the only question to ask is:
did I love?

Myself? Them?
In the moments. Across the days.
In subtle, gentle ways?

Nods to love, half-breaths, winks,
as well as the obvious leaps.

Never, did I give myself away?
That's not loving, that's wounding.

But an earnest look—did I love, when I could?
Did I choose to open, soften, let them in?

Did I see all the ways they too, ache?

Did I love? Myself and other—in balance.
Was I kind? As best I could be, given
circumstance?

Did I choose to see the best in them?
Not ignorantly, but genuinely.
Gently. Quietly.

Not as currency or bargaining tool.
Not as proof of my right to exist in the world
or to vie for God's approval.

Not because someone told me to,
or there's a script to follow,

but simply because I choose to.
I want to.

There will never be any awards given for it
but did I notice sameness in all of us?

Did I love today?

Just a simple, supple movement
—no matter what they saw in me.

Maybe it had to be from afar
—or in a way they couldn't see
and would never appreciate.

Maybe they were hard to love
but did I choose to love them, anyway?

Many will find this cliched
or saccharine—but it's everything.

And the other thing—
did I say "no" when "yes"
was not loving myself?

Was I true? Did I fill my own cells?

Put simply, when it came to it, did I try?
Did I really—really try—to open my heart

and love?

It's the only question ever worth asking

because it's the only answer
ever worth finding.

Lucy Grace

Human/More than Human

AS IF OUR HEARTS LIVE INSIDE OF US

As if we need a shrine to find devotion.
As if we have to leave our families
to wash the Guru's feet.

Or bank goodness
to earn God's intimacy.

As if love could be
contained in a temple,
the sacred found only in ritual.

As if orphans are
just in orphanages.

As if we are not ALL ministers,
preachers, teachers, thieves.

As if those being "healed"
aren't also the healers.

As if this world doesn't
undress us with its eyes,
bring us to our knees every time.

As if any one of us could ever claim
to know or unknow, this wonder.

As if every breath we ever drew
wasn't making love to possibility.

As if our spirit could ever be
separate, higher medicine than the
miracle of our beautiful, humanity.

GRACE

No matter what you have done,
do, or don't do—you are beloved.

Every single hair on your head is loved.

I know that repulses a part of you.
I know it frightens the shame-laden,
exiled orphans in you, but it does not
make it any less true.

You are, always have been
and always will be, completely
loved by existence.

Call it God, Great Spirit, Source, Awareness,
Consciousness or Allah—no matter.

Call it the breeze that blows through
all time, anointing your insides,
baptising the angles in you.

Call it the light that ignites
your blazing heart, shatters stars
and burns in all of us.

The point is you are wholly, exquisitely
loved—EXACTLY as you are.

It's not whether that's true, but whether
you can receive it. And when you glimpse this
—even for a moment—the entire cosmos sings
one long and deep hallelujah.
Choirs of flowers rejoice
and God shouts shots for the whole bar.

You are more than worthy.
Not due to any role you play,
not because of all your achievements
and accolades, not for the trophies you've
collected or all your endearments,
not for that perfect, beauty pageant score

and not because you haven't
completely fucked some things up,
wrestled with love, broken your own mind
and other people's hearts.

We all do that. That's human.

You have never had to earn God's love.
You already have it, simply because you exist.

God is not your critical father,
your withdrawing or smothering mother.

God is not the arseholes in high school
who made you feel invisible or
your brutal sibling—that live-in bully.

She is not the friends who abandoned you,
or the lover who opened your heart so deeply
and then betrayed you.

God is not human—we reduce Her to what we
are.

God is not the therapist who gave up on you,
or the boss who—no matter what—just can't see
you.

God has always been with you, of you, and for
you.

She is your greatest fan. Even when you're on
your knees, steeped in suffering, and calling Her
all manner of things.

Our deepest grief and confusion, is simply
nature's way of breaking us open and waking us
from the concussion we've been steeped in.

You were born worthy. And you'll die it too.

No matter what you are, aren't, do, or don't do.

FORGIVENESS IS

Not something that comes
from any outside source,
but from the pit of our own guts,
from the silken bile within us.

From us, for us.

From the softness and fullness
of holding all we are
                            and aren't
lightly.

We try here.
And we fall.

We rise, sometimes.

Let us hold our own hearts
like the most compassionate lover.
Humility, humour.

We are all in this
together.

SOMETIMES

We have to let things
play out like water.

All things flowing
unto each other.

The tides are not ours
to direct, or own.
Trying to outsmart the moon
is as foolish and futile as
waging war with ether.

All things become one another.
Each moment breathes the other.

This is.
I am.

There's only one way to go
give over, flow.

*

We have to become water.
Surrender to rock and eagre.
Take breath in ports,
harbours, watering places.

And when the seiche returns us,
to tidal madness, we learn to
let ourselves be submerged
and taught by the current.

It's inside the mystery and
confusion of sea swell,
that we find ground
to push against and

RISE.

We are water,
we are also endless

sky.

MY TEMPLE

Is not a body.
Not a building.
Not a shrine.

It is relationship.

In relationship I am
brought to my knees.

In relationship I see
all the things about me
I'd like to unsee.

It's easy to have grand
notions of who we are,
worshiping one another
from afar

but come close enough
that I may feel you breathing

this
this
this

is where awakening
is how we're moving.

I'VE BEEN THINKING ABOUT

All the ways we give ourselves away.
Death, in slow motion. How arteries harden.

Enslaving our light to culture and consumerism
seems too grand a notion in the face of
everyday addiction. It's our routine self-abandonments
that make up a life. These subtle giving overs:
a stifling here, shutting-down there
—so many angles of ourselves, filed down,
our edges held, and held, and held, like breath

until they burst out and destroy what they think
had them bound (the only light that was left).

*

And all the other ways, we give ourselves away.

Simple human things: a grin, to cover rage.

The way our hips beg to sway, but we ask them to
wait, and wait, and wait. (As if we have all the time

in the world—as if life isn't the deepest miracle.)

Longing, forced to stillness.
The dreams we don't dare let breathe us.

How much is giving over to God?
How much simply giving up?

A kind hand on the shoulder,
that really needed an honest mirror.

The lover we gave too much of ourselves to,
or not enough of ourselves for.

The everyday bullets we catch and bury
—more hardened arteries.

*

You find the light sometimes, but the romantic
notion of a bluebird stifled in your heart is really
just the old canary in a coalmine: desperate,
dying.

*

We carry our prisons within and recreate them
without.

And we are free. We have always been free.
But only insofar as we are conscious.

**Inspired by Charlies Bukowski's beautiful poem
"Bluebird."*

DON'T YOU SEE?

Your suffering is not your brokenness,
—it's your beauty.

There's no solution to our humanity.

All the ways we are tangled
and rumble through existence,

all the ways we try to reconcile
the opposing forces within us.

We are sea-glass, and sea.
Spirit, coming to terms with our humanity.
The being knows, but the mind has to catch up.

And there you are—looking so much like love,
tear-stained, hunched.

When I see your courage to be who you are,
to bow before the hollow bone of you, to try
and live inside the hauntings—like we all do,

YOU—cast the net of flesh wide.
You—render atoms, breath and marrow holy.
You—remind me
that the intelligence required is always

love.

COURAGE (NEW LIFE)

Can you hear the drum,
the drum, thrumming?

Calling through this baby,
hips swollen with maybes,

stretched-handed could-bes
unmanifest would-bes,
burning into being.

Our song is our work.

No matter what we do,
only who we are as we do it.

Spirit moves through us,

so rip open safety's womb and
drink, bare the wild teeth of wisdom,
for you are Delphi's woman
and in every breath you ever drew,
you were already named anew.

So throw back your head, arch
expectant breasts, open willing legs
Shiva's knife begs.

Let your blood gush freely.
Give yourself in ecstasy

BIRTH!

YOUR BODY IS NATURE

Waves, particle, plasma.

Ever heard of those scientists
who speak cruelly to plants,
then measure them wilting?

Or speak to them lovingly and
measure them growing?

YOU are those plants.
YOU are leaves, airwaves and
mud. Your heart was carved in
myth, ache and stars.

Every atom of you is a universe
spinning on the hinges
of arterial-tides and words,
so anoint yourself with every thought—
we shape light with our words.

What do you think happens
when you curse the body you're in?

Or when you let another focus their
steaming self-hatred in your direction?

What happens in our cells
when we cast judgment out to another?
It travels through US first.

Guilt, shame, perfection—it's poison.

*

We've been raised to reject ourselves,
dismantle, abhor and minimise ourselves

but here's the miracle: when we look with a
gaze of celebration—we find things to love.

When we look with a gaze determined to hate
we find lack—always.

To be in love with your body, is to be
in love with nature. If plants wither
in the face of hatred, it's time to enter a
consensual relationship—with our flesh.

The galaxy of you was made to blow stars
through open sky, so don't look back
—despite your too-short legs, too long arms,
too thin hair, too broken heart.

Take every midnight of you and surround it with
love.

We are moonbeams and pretty things
as well as phlegm and grief.

Extraordinary beauty is found in the "ordinary"
—so soften the energy it takes to reject yourself.

You blow hearts apart, just by being who you are.
The sun does that. But so does moon and shadow.

Thank God for all of you.

Others may forget it, culture may condemn it,
but don't you ever let yourself
unlearn your own magic.

*

Prayer is an atmosphere.
It's not reserved for when we're
on our knees—speaking.

It's all of us, moving.

*

And long may we know
our bodies as

holy.

I WENT TO GOD ON MY KNEES

And She told me to rise.

She said: "Child, you can't serve me
AND your fear. Let the summoners
drum, beat your name into path and prayer.

This is uncompromising deep light. Ascent.
No gentle incline, like that from winter
to sun, but a monumental moving
of axis and bend.

This is not fever, this is the gnosis of solstice.
Our essence is elemental, and it burns
through every breath of us.

This is moon and magma.

So pick up your axe and chop.
This is your time for silence.
And this is your time for work.
You need wood for the fires you're

burning into being in."

ON BEAUTY

We see in "other" what we see
in ourselves.
Beauty or brokenness.
A problem to be fixed, tolerated.
Or the unique curve of a butterfly's wing,
the smoke-flesh span of you,
a miracle drifting.

Skin, shapeshifting.

*

We see "other" not as they are
but as WE are.
We see: in a face, in a body,
only holographic knowing.

Holy or unholy, depending on
self-understanding (or self-loathing.)

It all comes back, our limitation, or clarity
—to bind, or free US.
This is why, when we love,
we love ourselves first and most.

We think we love for others' benefit,
but loves-mist starts in the pit of our guts
—it fills OUR cells first before travelling
outward.

The same can be said for judgement.

ONCE WE WERE WARRIORS

We mined all the parts of our lives
we deemed inadequate, for excavating,

cutting and pasting ourselves.
Perfecting. Levelling. Proving.
Master-minding.

Now we know differently. Now
we KNOW we are poetry dancing
and poetry contains everything.

We are Grace, shapeshifting.

Now we anoint everything,
we know all of us is holy.

We are light AND the shadow
cast by it. We are sacred mess.
Sublime, perfect process.

*

I am.
This body.

And I am
your body.

I am cosmic.
I am human.

I am individual
and I am union.

The end of suffering
is not benign perfection

the end of suffering
is forgiveness—laughter—
at my own fumbling humanity.

There is such exquisite beauty
in all of me.

*

Don't you see?

You were never an apology.

*

Galaxies alight in your eyes
no matter the wars you wage,
the places you stay stuck, the angles
of you, the plain exhaustion at your own
imperfection, the ways you misattune
to those you love,
the way no one seems to hold you
in quite the way you want.

You
have never been an apology.
Your heart is vast enough to dance
with asteroids and stars.

You are full weightless-gravity.
Cosmic, yes,
but that has never been separate,
higher medicine, than the magnificence
of your beautiful, bumbling

humanity.

THIS IS FIERCE GRACE

Ablaze through mantle, iron and nickel.
It runs from earth core to crust,
through trees, broken promises, tar.

This Grace spirits the lust in us.
Hallows every nail hammered
to the lonely crosses in us.

We are palms-up tender, we are
here, but we are more than human.

We are the poem.

*

In this life, we don't have a map,
but we do have a compass.
Our body tells us which way to go.

And isn't God a roach too?

The hollow bone of us. The un-touched,
un-played instruments of us.

Every longing, muddied oil spill, leaking
in the sea of us—comes home to love.

*

The echoes no one seems to hear.

Lucy Grace

The ways we reach for ground
in the dark. And yet Grace

is what we are.

WE MEET THE GURU IN LIFE

In a child's eyes, or some dime-store cowboy
chancing his luck, with our blazing heart.

The curriculum is love. The education, life.

We are taught by sea-storms and coastlines,
broken hearts and lighthouses, fogged in the distance.
We train our eyes over time to recognise them,
learn to scan the horizon, make choices.

Work to resist pallid instructions, sold to us by
a culture who doesn't remember
the intelligence required is always love,

the practice, giving over to slipstreams,
when they come.

*

In this life, we don't have a map, but we do
have a compass. We use our hearts to chart
course, lose ourselves sometimes in scenic
detours and maelstroms.

Stand bravely and completely at the helm,
give ourselves deeply to current and wind,
—let THEM teach us, what THEY will.

And when all else stills,
the only question to ask is
did I love well?

*

When navigating, there's one thing we can be sure of:
when the way says "yes" —it's Grace.
And when the way says "no"—it's even deeper Grace.

A WOMAN'S BODY

Is a community commodity.

We teach her to abhor
the fullness of herself,
in much the same way
we despise our mothers
for never having loved us

into wholeness.

It's rare to see a full-bodied woman
aglow with the deliciousness
of her curves, knowing deeply that
her rounded hips are God in flesh.

Her smile as wide and laden
as the sway of full, free breasts.

A woman who eats nuts with abandon
and licks cream from her lips.

We've been taught to punish
the milk maid, to drench her in shame.

Her body was our first home
and we hate her for casting us from it,
so you can be damn sure
we'll try to repossess it.

We're still steeped in resentment
from the moment she unclenched us
from her bleeding teet.

We're still enraged
over our desperate need
for her to love us enough that
we are finally complete,

so we'll claim victory
over her body—by robbing her
of the pleasure of its full glory.

We'll imprison her in impossible
expectations and choke-holds
and call them "standards."

Her undernourished physical form
is just a mirror for all the ways
our hearts are in famine.

We all long to return
to that womb of safety

to bask, once again in Her
reverence, Her attention, Her
unflinching devotion.

We despise her
for not being our solution
to separation from God,
so we reduce her hips, her
thighs, her lips, her lashes
to impossible mathematics,

then convince her to agree with us.

We reduce her body to a child's body.
Ask her to starve herself, demand she
disappear into a waif-like-wisp of herself

or else

pump up her bottom and clinch her waist
to cartoon-like veracity, minimise her
to a caricature of herself—and call it a BBL.

We teach her that her body
is either an apology—or currency.

It's a hard truth to hear, but we want
our women weak, frail, scared.

In every way we want
to reduce them to at least
half the magic
half the freedom
half the power they truly are

so we can finally feel some
semblance of control
over our fear
of our deep need of THEIR

love.

Lucy Grace

WHEN WE SEE THE GOOD

In each other, we call it forth.

Try it—look for light
and you will find light.

Look to celebrate
and you will find reason.

Radiance is everywhere,
buried inside the grumpiest
among us, like a pearl in mud
even more glorious
for the surprise of finding it.

There's no one too small
for light—it's what we are.

People aren't "bad." They're
just different scales of wounded-
creating more,

they've just forgotten themselves
for a bit, and when we see
their sacredness

we summon it.

ON PARENTING

PRAYERS

Are not found
in bricks and mortar,

in pinched faces
looking over shoulders.

Prayers are formed
in the bile of my belly
when I'm on my knees
cleaning gunk off the floor
under your chair.

What a prayer!

If I can't love you here—now,
then how can I say I love?

Prayers are formed in the heady
gratitude of sun-song, in the
murky blackness that I am.

God is the sway of my hips
and these bleeding breasts.

It's here I worship: at your tiny feet,
broken open and becoming.

Exhaustion, grief and surrender.

God is the mist in me
I am more than this
                    weather.

Lucy Grace

THANK YOU

I walked
a thousand blocks

with bleeding feet

for you to teach me
how to unlearn everything.

And in all those moments
when I was a refugee
from myself, despair blinding

you stood quietly, green eyes
firing, willing me through.

I suppose letting you rewire
me, was never gonna be easy,
but in the unravelling
a sacred rebuilding.

You: braided into me.

And all the distraction, the numbing
the ceaseless running of before:
given over (willingly or forced)
to the quiet that you require.
The laser-beam-present-moment focus
of watching a snail inch along a path
for an hour, together.

The subtle strength of holding myself
still-fast enough for you
each day anew.

*

They say parenting is the fastest route
to enlightenment, if we can transcend
all the frightened parts of ourselves.

But I was never logic's daughter, could never
muster lust, for any idea of a saviour,

have always preferred giving over to water
when the maelstroms come.

*

We are all haunted, grace-filled beings
—I was just trying to live with the hauntings,

wasn't seeking, anything.

But you brought me to my knees, you broke me
bodily (the heart was just the half of it.)

You opened me,
white flagged the wars in me.
My three-foot guru, in gumboot feet.

*

When the light comes,
it spares nothing.

*

Rose
you were sent to improve me
and I thank God for your love.

I thank God I had the sense
to let you undo me.

Lucy Grace

MY DEEPEST WORK

Is not to stand
on some grand stage
and talk about expansion
into vaster spiritual states.

It's not to inflate
my sense of knowing or
doing, anything.

It's not to write books
that simply teach myself
all of the lessons that are
still undone in my system.

It's not to pray for collective
trauma to be unknotted.

For wisdom to be channelled.
For the weather of my life to be
predicted or managed.

It's no technique.
No trick.
No trance.
No acrobatics.

I do not need to contort
myself into some perfect asana.

Read every tradition
cover to cover.

It's not calling in the Goddess
or finding another role
in priestess, it's not transcendence
or embodied catharsis.

It's no pilgrimage away from—this.

Though these things can be of value,
my deepest work is silent, subtle,
invisible, immeasurable.

I am here to love you.

Deeply, completely.
And it's the hardest thing I'll ever do.
It's an arbitrary expanse of measures:
seconds. nights. inches.

When I'm exhausted.
When I'm selfish.
When I'm empty.
When I'm trudging through rain
and you need sweetness.
When we're up in the night
and you need patience.

This is so much harder
than ten days of Vipassana.

This coming together

is crawling on knees,
bruised knuckles, life's shrapnel
flying around my hearts
emptiest trenches.

The need in your green eyes
is the frontline.

So what I do here
—when no one is looking—
IS my dharma.

No Zen Master
will ever be as demanding
as a five-year old with fever.

No love holds this ability
to destroy me, if I am fearless enough
to walk into it completely.

Can I let love own me?

Rose, you were sent to improve me,
so I'll keep trying to let you undo me

to let love move through me
and infuse the deserted
battlefields in me.

I'll keep trying to find humour,
surrender, humility—instead of armour.

And in these moments when I want to run,
when I feel the weight of suffocation threaten

let me remember

I
asked
for
this.

I asked to learn how
to love, so deeply, so purely
that I would forget myself.

I asked to be broken open,
I asked to know the meaning
of true devotion.

So God gave me you.

Not a mountain, not a nun's habit,
not a secret sect, not dusty crypts
and relics—God gave me you,
a live-in guru.

God gave me my need
for autonomy, this fear of
consumption, and every single
want you lay at my feet.

So I will keep trying to soften
lay down my protection

open
open
open.

I will keep trying to give myself away
to your love's wisdom.

Fall into the risk
of surrender's abyss.

Meet love's edge, and expand it.

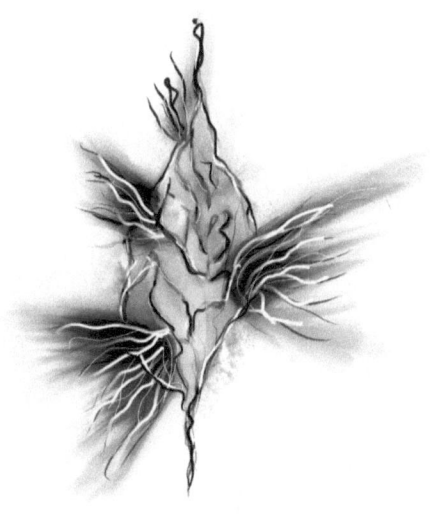

Acknowledgements

Anything that I may be,
is owed to the multitude of beings
who have loved, and love me.

Love, is the only lasting thing.
It stays with us
long after everything else leaves.

There are a billion ways to love:
patience, kindness, listening.
Our tears can be love. Our true seeing.

But we can't love at speed.

Let us slow down, inhabit
the flesh we're in

know sinew, cell, quark
fill marrow, atom, lung-heart.

*

Let me start by thanking those in flesh.

First and foremost, the deepest thank you to my mother, Heather Grace. Your unconditional love has buoyed and strengthened me. It is the scaffolding my life has stood on. The years upon years of telling me that you love me "no matter what you do, became or are - in any given moment" left a deep sense of my inherent lovability, worthiness and voice. As well as the ability to carve my own path, separate from what others may think. What an immense inheritance – thank you. Your spirit, prayers and blessings have filled and strengthened me in ways both of us will never truly know. You have taught me to love others and myself with forgiveness, grace and trying to see the best always. Thank you for everything.

Rose, my precious daughter – you have been my greatest teacher, my guru. Those are not just words. Nothing could ever express how you have opened me, deepened me, and been the reckoning this body-mind needed. You are the greatest gift of my life and I will be grateful to you, always. You are, and will remain my deepest love. Part of me – always.

Pam and Daryl, you have shepherded **me**, stood by me, nurtured me and held me through my whole life. You have been pillars of support and strength, standing close – but never with force – so I've always known that should I fall, someone would be there to catch me, which has given me immense courage. You have strengthened me, encouraged me and held me - and your voice of celebration and encouragement, lives inside me now as my own.

Kallie and Ben, you are my siblings not in blood, but in what matters – heart. You have always been willing to see the best in me, and support me when I have needed you. We have watched each other grow up, you are part of my deepest heart and I will love and respect you both forever.

And my friends – my chosen family, the ones who witness me into existence – who see my goodness, my light and share theirs with me. You hold me, enrich my life deeply and nourish this precious life-force that it may grow and grow and grow. I won't name you individually but you do know who you are. Thank you, for walking beside me. I am eternally grateful for all that you teach and gift me. And for your deep support and encouragement with these poems, and your enjoyment of them.

To David Tensen for your patience and humility while working with me on this book. You are the teaching. It has been a huge undertaking, and you have never once complained (when having every right to) but instead have taken everything in your stead with the grace and heart of a true warrior. I am so grateful for that, and for you. What an honour to work together, and to know such a steadfast, reliable, honest and just plain kind, man. The wisdom, and humility of you moves me deeply.

To Bryan Borland, my dear friend, but also my editor – how can words describe how you have supported me, lifted me and encouraged me on this journey. The day you sent me a message saying "I am so proud of you! I wonder what would the little girl think now, you've come all this way, and written a book." I cried hard and soft and long and deep. Thank you for seeing me, and treasuring all the Russian dolls of me with your seeing. You are a walking heart. And how I got so lucky to have you walking with me, is beyond me. But I'm sure glad I did.

To Chelan Harkin, my sister. You have been on this journey since it was first dreamed up. You have midwifed the author in me, cherished my heart and musings, laughed with me, cried with me – supported my voice and championed my ideas. Our voices are so intertwined now, you live through me and I through you. You are truly what we dream friends will be and I am so grateful to have you by my side on this journey. Thank you, for being.

To Riyaz Motan, one of the most beautiful men I have ever met. Thank you for teaching me how to be a friend. For standing by me, always. Checking on me, celebrating my wins, and holding my tears. For listening to my long-winded recounts of dreams and for letting me hold you too, that I may know myself as wisdom and strength. AND despite having stage four lung cancer, doing absolutely everything in your power to support this book. I am blown apart by you. I adore you. You are my teacher and family.

To Uliai Williams for your ever present support and encouragement. Both of the practical kind (a cottage to live and write in for a month away from my duties) and of the heart kind – all the ways you shout from the rooftops your love of poetry and the arts, champion them, and include mine in that. I am so very grateful for your holding and generous heart, thank you.

To the artists who contributed to this book Kira Kirova (kirasheart.com) who wove her magic on the cover and did the beautiful line drawings. Dan Hillier (danhillier.com) who contributed 'Ground' and Robby Donaghey (ArtisticGenius.com) who contributed 'Yeshua.' I am eternally grateful for your hearts work and the depth and beauty you have brought to this book, thank you.

And to you, dear reader. Without you, this book would never have come through me. It has all been for you.

My deepest wish is that these poems find hearts to embed themselves in that need reminding of their inherent beauty, worth and might.

I hope these words bring comfort and inspiration to tired feet. And remind people of all the beauty in the sacred mess of being human (and so much more than human.)

I hope they wrap around cold shoulders, nuzzle into necks and fill broken hearts. I hope these words bring joy and relief wherever they go and inspire people to dance their precious lives deeply. And most of all I hope they fill everyone they reach with a sense of how deeply loved by existence they are – exactly as they are.

Now for the unseen among us, but so deeply felt.

Thank you, most deeply, to God. The deep heart of existence that has been so keenly felt all my life. That lives through me and breathes through me and for whom I would die over and over, just to know the joy of being used by you in this life. Thank you for loving me and teaching me and roaring your laughter through this belly, these feet, these hands, these...words. I want nothing more than for you to keep taking this vessel and leading it where you see fit. Thank you for dancing me so deeply. And for loving me so earnestly. Thank you for writing through me.

Thank you to the light beings – ancestors and guides - who walk with me, stand guard and strengthen me, teach and cherish me. There are no words I could say that can serve to express my gratitude for your shepherding. And for the simple joy of knowing you, and being known by you. No matter what, you have never left. If I have to walk up a mountain, you come too.

Just being beside me is enough, but all the help, all the guidance, all the love – is a balm to this earth school, you are my family, only occasionally seen with the eyes, but so deeply cherished and felt with the heart.

Finally, thank you to the earth – the Mother - to Waiheke Island, my home. This benevolent being, that homes me, holds me, gives ground under me, teaches me, sings to me, reminds me, mirrors me, co-regulates with me. And gives so much of herself that I may have the chance to express fully and deeply and know myself like light – full spectrum. A deep thank you, for your unconditional service and love.

www.ingramcontent.com/pod-product-compliance
Lightning Source LLC
Chambersburg PA
CBHW022012290426
44109CB00015B/1153